For Joe
M·E·

For Roger
G· R·

First American edition published in 1997 by
Crocodile Books, USA
An imprint of Interlink Publishing Group, Inc.
99 Seventh Avenue, Brooklyn, New York 11215
Text © by Mark Ezra 1997
Illustrations © by Gavin Rowe 1997

Published simultaneously in Great Britain by Magi Publications.

Library of Congress Cataloging-in-Publication Data

Ezra, Mark.
    The frightened little owl / Mark Ezra ; pictures by Gavin Rowe. -- 1st
American ed.
      p. cm.
    Summary: Although afraid to fly, Little Owl leaves the safety of her nest
and goes to look for her missing mother, who has been watching over her all
the time.
    ISBN 1-56656-264-3 (hardcover)
1. Owls--Juvenile fiction. [1. Owls--Fiction. 2. Flight--Fiction.]
I. Rowe, Gavin, ill. II. Title.
PZ10.3.E98Fr   1997
[E]--dc21   96-50357
                                           CIP
                                           AC

Printed and bound in Belgium
10 9 8 7 6 5 4 3 2 1

MARK EZRA

The Frightened
Little Owl

pictures by GAVIN ROWE

Crocodile Books, USA

An imprint of Interlink Publishing Group, Inc.
NEW YORK

Snug in a nest in the tallest tree sat Little Owl, who looked like a feathery ball with big, golden eyes. Each night she watched her mother spread her wings and glide silently over the treetops to hunt for food.

Little Owl always felt alone and afraid as she
waited for her mother to come home. All she
could hear outside the nest was the rustling
of branches and the howling of wind.

The world seemed a cold and frightening place.
Little Owl tugged at the soft lining of the nest
with her beak and wrapped it close around her.
It made her feel safe.

"You'll soon be able to fly like me," said Little Owl's mother one day. "Just imagine how wonderful it will feel when you can soar silently in the night with the wind beneath your wings!"

"But I don't *want* to fly," cried Little Owl. "It's scary out there. I want to stay here in my nest forever."

And she nestled down into the hole again.

"Come with me, Little Owl," said Mother Owl
one evening. "Come and choose your own supper
tonight. You'll enjoy that!"
Little Owl scrambled after her mother onto a
branch, but when she saw how far it was to the
ground, she felt dizzy.
"I *never* want to fly!" Little Owl cried, as she edged
her way back into the nest.
And Mother Owl flew
off alone.

Little Owl snuggled down and waited for her supper. Outside in the woods the sun set and the moon came out. Little Owl began to feel hungry, but there was no sign of her mother. Surely she should have been back by now.

Little Owl was very worried.
What if something awful had
happened to her mother?

Little Owl plucked up all her courage and hopped out onto the branch. Somehow she felt less dizzy than she had before, and the ground didn't seem so far away. Trembling, she took another step . . .

. . . and at that moment a terrific
gust of wind sprang up. Suddenly
Little Owl lost her footing.

The next thing she knew she was tumbling through the air. Without thinking, she spread her wings –

and she was flying!
Flapping madly, Little Owl tried to reach her own branch, but the wind was too strong, and she was buffeted to earth.

"Ouch!" cried Little Owl,
as she hit the ground.
"Well, that wasn't bad for a beginner," said
a voice nearby. "Why don't you try again?"
Little Owl looked up and saw a young fawn.
"I don't *want* to fly," cried Little Owl.
"I want my mother! She's flown
away, and I'm scared that she
won't come back!"
"I bet she will," said the fawn.
"If you listen, you'll hear her."

And sure enough, from far away across the trees,
Little Owl heard a familiar sound.
"*Kiew! Kiew!*"

"Yes, that's her!" cried Little Owl in excitement.
Saying goodbye to the fawn, she ran and flapped
across the glade.

"Mother! Mother!" cried Little Owl, and before
she knew it she was flying!
"Well done!" the fawn called out as Little Owl
rose higher and higher into the air.

The young owl flew on, but her mother
always seemed to be just ahead of her.

"Mother! Mother!" sobbed Little Owl.
"Wait for me! Don't fly off again." She began
to feel she would never catch up.

In her hurry and fright Little Owl bumped into
a tree. She fell to the ground, disturbing a family
of mice who were out looking for supper.
"Run!" screamed Mother Mouse to her babies.
"Run, it's an owl!"
There was a scuffle
of tiny paws, and
the mice vanished.

It was very quiet in the woods now, and Little Owl felt dreadfully alone. She gave a small sob. Perhaps her mother had gone away forever?

"MOTHER," she shrieked, "WHERE ARE YOU?"

"I'm right here," said a familiar voice above Little Owl's head. "You didn't really think I would leave you, did you? I've been watching over you all the time, hoping you would fly. And now you can. Well done, Little Owl!"

Little Owl blinked. Yes, she *could* fly! She gave a hoot of delight, spread her wings and flew around and around the glade. She dipped and soared towards the morning sky. Her mother was right! Flying *was* wonderful!